T0245627

THIS IS THE
STORY
OF
BLACKY
THE CAT

Russell Allison

This is the Story of Blacky the Cat
2nd Edition
©2024 Russell Allison
Illustrated by Lenora Allison

ISBN 979-8-35094-485-3

CONTENTS

THIS IS THE STORY OF BLACKY THE CAT

The cat that saved a cat family, and maybe me too, and took us all to the Kittie Kat Ranch !!!

My name is Rusty. I was an Orthopaedic Surgeon in a solo private practice in Russellville, Arkansas, for 25 years. The people that worked with me were the best. They were so kind and sweet and willing to help. I loved my practice and my patients but as the climate of medicine changed, it became impossible to keep my doors open.

I closed my private practice and took a job as a hospital employee in Coffeyville, Kansas. This is how Blacky came into my life……

COFFEYVILLE

Coffeyville was a very poor town. It is full of run down homes and streets. I found the people there to be kind and outgoing. Although they had very little, they were willing to give all they had and work hard to help in any way possible. To this day I continue to communicate with many of my former co-workers. They are not my co-workers they are my friends.

The town was full of stray cats. I would see them everywhere while driving around the town. All sizes and shapes and colors. But they all had one thing in common. This "look" in their eyes. It's hard to describe. Desperation, fear, hunger, hopelessness, all. It said to everyone, don't come close to me, I don't trust you !!!

They would dart like lightning from one hiding site to another. Knowing any day could be their last. They would seem so cold in the winter and so hot in the summer.

I was never a cat person. In fact, I could not stand them. I could not imagine why anyone would want a cat, especially in their house. I grew up on a ranch in Arkansas, and we had horses and dogs and cattle, not cats!!!!

THE HOUSE

I bought a small house in Coffeyville across the street from the hospital. It was a cute little house. I would walk back and forth to work each day. It had been remodeled on the outside with aluminum siding and new windows. It had a covered porch on the side of the house and a double glass door that led into and out of the house (only one side actually opened). There were two steps on the porch that led down to a concrete patio. I had a small table and two fold out camping style chairs on that patio. I would have to pour the water out of the seats every time it rained. There was also a Blackstone gridle and an old T post that had been used to dry clothes in the past. I used it to hang flowerpots in the spring and summer. That patio led to a detached two car garage. A chain link fence surrounded my yard to the side of the garage. A single tree, a bricked burning barrel and a Martin house were all that were in my yard.

I was told the house had belonged to an elderly lady who had been moved to a nursing home. She had believed she would return home one day so the home was just as she left it. Fully furnished, right down to her walking cane, still hanging on her rocking chair. Unfortunately, she never made it back to her home.

One of the part time nurses in the OR overheard me telling someone that I had bought that house. She told me that that was her great aunt's home. She informed me that there were many family members that could have used that furniture. So, I gave it all away to the family members. I hope it went somewhere special. I worry about her cane more than anything. I could just feel that was special to her.

I moved into the house. My wife decorated it beautifully. She used furniture that had been in storage. A chair and a painting of Indians doing the "Buffalo Dance" that had been in my son's room when he was in high school. I hung that painting above my fireplace and put that chair in the living room. There was a nice round table that had been sitting upside down in our garage in Arkansas for several years. One of its legs had been broken. I repaired the leg, and it went nicely in the dining area with two old armchairs which my wife had had recovered.

The kitchen was old. There were old wooden cabinets along one wall. Some of the doors would not stay closed all the way. There was a single sink in the middle with no garbage disposal. On the other wall was a stand-alone gas stove and cook top. Across from the stove, on the other wall, was a single white over and under refrigerator/freezer. The white paint on the front of the refrigerator was wearing off and rust could be seen beneath. However, it worked just fine.

THE PLAN

Living in Coffeyville was good and working out pretty well. My wife was coming up to Coffeyville some during the week and I would go home to Arkansas about every other weekend. But as time went by, she came less and less. You see when I moved to Kansas, we had one granddaughter. But within the first 6 months of being there we were up to three granddaughters !! She was simply too busy helping with the granddaughters to come to Kansas.

I enjoyed my walk to work each morning. I liked the people I worked with and my patients. I enjoyed the walk home. But in the evenings, sitting alone in my little house, it was lonely. So, I decided to find things to do in the evening to tie up my time. One of these things was picking up food to go and bringing it home. I could eat it while watching the evening news on television. Monday night was pizza night, Tuesday night was

Kentucky Fried Chicken, Wednesday was Barb B Q, Thursday was The Yoke, a local bar in town that had the best hamburgers and fries. Friday and Saturday were open since I usually went back to Arkansas. On Sunday night my good friend and sales rep for many years, Troy Boudreaux, would come up from Arkansas. We would drive up to Independence, Kansas, and eat at a little restaurant called Stoney's Grub and Pub. All the people knew us by name. They had our table saved. Even the two cooks would come out and say hello.

You'll remember from the description of my kitchen that it did not have a garbage disposal. So, I was raking the leftovers into the kitchen trash can every night so that I could wash my dishes. I washed my dishes every night so I could have a fresh coffee pot in the morning.

One night I decided to rake all of the leftovers onto a paper plate. It was a Tuesday, so I had been to Kentucky Fried Chicken. I hated wasting the leftovers. I thought, there are lots of hungry stray animals out there, maybe something would eat the leftovers. I took the plate out the glass door, onto the porch, down the two steps onto the concrete patio, then all the way to the back of the patio and set it down between the free standing garage and the house.

The next morning, I walked out onto the porch to go to work. I noticed the paper plate was still there, but everything else was gone, except the bones. They had been picked clean. I threw the bones in the outdoor trash can and went on about my day.

LOOKING FOR THOSE CATS!!!

I began to put my leftovers out each night and they were always gone the next morning when I left for work. I never saw what was eating them. I never knew when they came or when they left.

So, I decided to replace my outdoor light on my side covered porch with a motion detector light. I would point the sensor toward the plate. For weeks the light would come on. I would run to the door, and nothing would be there. Finally, I decided to move the paper plate up the steps. First one step, then two. The food was always gone, but who?? Finally, I put the paper plate with the leftovers on it on the porch in front of the glass doors. This was the first time, after a year of trying, I saw the Kitty Kats!!!!!

Patience, that can be difficult at times. The old saying, "good things come to those who wait", is not always true. But the saying, "I want it and want it now", almost never works. A full year of being patient was well worth it to finally see those cats and begin a relationship with them.

BUILDING TRUST

My couch, where I watched TV, was about 20 feet from those glass doors. When the lights came on, I knew the cats were there. But if I even stood up, they were gone. Remember, don't come close to me, I don't trust you !!!

So it began, somewhat of a game to us. I was determined to win those Kitty Kats over. Troy would come on Sunday nights. He was as determined to get close to those cats as I was. He would lay down on his belly and crawl toward that door. It took several weeks before he could get to that door and watch them through the glass. Remember, this is an almost sixty year old man, crawling on his belly to get close to see those Kiddy Kats. It was so funny to watch. They would run so quickly.

Remember, I was working on this every night. Patiently.

Once they got use to the lights there were three cats that came up every night.

Boots who had four white stocking feet. He was the biggest and prettiest of all the cats. But also the most untrusting and the quickest to run away.

Calico was a calico cat and she had beautiful white and yellow and dark fur. She seemed to want to believe and trust, but she just could not give in to trust and love. I think she had just seen too much evil to believe. I actually tried to touch her once and she hissed at me.

And Blacky, who was a black cat with a little bit of white fur on her chest and huge yellow eyes. She had the deepest and loudest "meow" I had ever heard. She too had that look of desperation, fear, hunger and hopelessness. She too would run at the slightest notion of harm or entrapment.

Other cats would occasionally join them but these three seemed to be somewhat of a pack.

TRUST

Trust, trust is so hard to build. One slip of that trust can take months or even years to heal. It may never go away completely, and it may take a lifetime of work. It doesn't matter if it is with cats, people, horses, dogs or any other creature. If they cannot trust you, they cannot love you, and cannot be comfortable around you. I had learned that through my own life, and I tried to apply this to these cats.

I bought regular cat food. I put a 25 pound bag of dry food in the detached two car garage. I wanted to make sure they had something to eat every night. As the winter set in, and it was dark early, sometimes I would come home and they would be waiting on me. They were hungry. But they would be sitting on the fence so that they could get away if needed. They knew I would feed them, but they still could not completely trust me.

CALICO'S KITTENS

Although I fed them every night. It had almost been two years. Progress was so slow.

I had come to love these cats so much. Remember, I had hated cats before, and now they were starting to show signs of loving me back. But it seems like that sometimes. You come to love someone and you long for them to respond and it just doesn't happen when you want it to. It seems you've wasted all the emotion for nothing. But love is never really wasted.

By this time, I had gained some trust. It was springtime and I could actually sit at the end of the porch on a fold up camping type chair and the cats would come eat. I still could not touch any of them. But I think they could tell that I cared about them. That I would never hurt them. I felt like I was making progress.

Sometimes you can love someone so much, but they just don't trust, and continue to be an alley cat. They are too afraid to believe, and you may have helped place that fear in them.

Then one night, I was asleep in my bed, and I was awoken by noise. I went to the back glass door by the porch and there was Calico with a bunch of calico kittens. She had had baby kittens !!! They seemed to be everywhere. They had to be several weeks old. It was late, as if she did not want to bring them out too early. They seemed so happy, and so hungry, they were eating everything.

Every week I saw less and less of those kittens. The last time I saw Calico there was one last kitten with her. I think the streets had taken them. Baby kittens don't have much hope of living out on the streets at night. I wished so badly Calico could have loved and trusted me. I would have been so glad to have loved and cared for all of those calico Kittie Kats.

Trust is so hard to build once it has been broken. I think she had seen too much to believe.

BLACKY IS BRAVE

By now it was spring and the air was cool so I began to leave the back glass door open. One night, Blacky just walked into the house and sat down on the floor beside me.

The next night she came into the house through the open glass back door and jumped up into my lap. She just sat down, like it was normal. From that night on, she was my cat, and I belonged to her. I had never even liked a cat. She would sit in my lap and my wife would call to face time me on our cell phones. Blackly would take her paw and push the phone away. Saying, no, he is mine, you can't have him.

Can you imagine how brave that was for this cat. She had been disappointed so many times. One more disappointment may have been too much. But she was brave and took that chance.

It's kind of like when I met my wife. We had just met and we were at a friend's house. I was sitting in a chair with large pillow arms. She just came over and sat down on the arm of the chair I was sitting on. I just fell into a million pieces. Oh my God !!! Did this girl of my dreams just sit down next to me !!! She could have just sat somewhere else. I could have said "excuse me, this is my chair". I could have missed the love of my life. But she was brave and took that chance, just like Blacky.

It's funny, I never saw that look in Blacky's eyes again. No desperation, fear, hunger or hopelessness. She knew she was my cat, and I belonged to her. Just like that girl knew, I would become her husband and always belong to her.

But Blacky would still go to the glass door and meow each night. Wanting to go out for the night. That was still her life. At heart, she was still an alley cat.

BLACKY HAS KITTEN'S

Blacky seemed to gain weight. Again, I had never been around a cat, so I didn't understand. Then, all of a sudden, she was really thin. I thought she might have had kittens. But where were they ???? I tried following her day after day, but she would lose me.

Then one day she left and was on top of the chain link fence. You remember, it went to the yard to the side of my detached two car garage. She jumped off and went under a bush in my neighbor's back yard.

Although I should not have, I went around the fence and through the gate into my neighbor's back yard, without permission. I lifted up the branches and there they were. Five Little Baby Kittie Kats !!!

They could not have been more than a few days old. I tried to leave them alone. But I made the mistake of speaking to them. They started to follow my voice. I ran around the chain link fence to the gate and into my own yard. But when I got to my yard, here they came. Working their way through that chain link fence !!! They just would not quit following me !!!

I knew that they would not survive and wind up like Calico's kittens. So, I gathered them up and put them in a box in the back room by the glass door that led to the porch. I left the glass door open so Blacky could come in.

I sat down on my couch to breathe, and gather myself as to what had just happened. What would I possibly do with baby Kitty Kat's? Then, all of a sudden, here came Blacky. She had one of those baby Kiddie Kat's with her. She had it in her mouth, picked up by the nap of its neck. She had decided they should be in the guest bedroom on the rug. She carried all five of them back to that guest bedroom one at a time and placed them on the rug. And that's where they stayed and where Blacky would raise them.

RAISING BABY KITTIE KATS

I kept the door closed to the spare bedroom at all times except when Blacky wanted in or out. I would go into their room every morning before work and then again after work and lay down on the rug with them and sing to them, so they would know my voice.

That simple act of singing to them would play out to be a big part of their future.

I bought a cat litter box and cat litter. I bought a self feeder of dry food and an automatic watering device so they could eat and drink when I was at work. Remember, I didn't even like cats in the past. Now here they were, in my house !!! They were getting bigger and stronger. They used that cat litter box and there was never cat poop on the floor. But man!!!! Five baby Kitties Kat's poop a lot in a litter box and I had to clean it every day !!!!!

GOOD PEOPLE

I would have to go back to Arkansas on the weekends to see my wife and children and granddaughters. I was so fortunate to know Rachelle. She was a scrub tech in the operating room with me and also worked at The Yoke. After every case she would say "Thank you Dr Allison" and I would say "No, thank you Rachelle".

Rachelle had been a burn victim. So, she would leave each year to go to Burn Camp. She loved taking care of kids that had been burned. She is one of those "good people" that are so hard to find. She offered to take those baby Kittie Kats and Blacky home with her and her family on the weekends when I would go back to Arkansas. They just lived a few blocks away.

See, we talked about this earlier. Trust, Rachelle and her family are just "good people". You can not just find that anywhere. Trust, I knew she and her family could be trusted. She and her family were willing to take on a burden they did not need or could not afford. They kept those cats for more weekends than I can count. I am so thankful for her and her family.

THE MOVE

My contract with Coffeyville was up and it was time to move home to Arkansas. What to do with all these cats?? Several of the girls I worked with in the OR offered to take some. Rachelle volunteered to take them all, and give them away to good homes. But they still needed Blacky for milk. She was my cat, and I wasn't leaving her to go back to the streets. She could not be disappointed again.

I had made a commitment to Blacky. I had promised her that I would take care of her and she would never have to live on the streets again. She would never have to feel desperation, fear, hunger or hopelessness. And I always keep my word.

You see, in life, all you really have that separates the honest people from the rest is their word. If you agree to do something, you do it, that's keeping your word. If you agree to do something and you don't do it, you have broken your word. Once you have broken your word you can no longer be trusted. And we have talked about how important trust is and how hard it is to restore.

So, we moved back to Arkansas. I didn't have to hire movers. I had made such great friends that they showed up to help without even asking. Randy, who was an x-ray tech at the hospital who had become my closest friend in Coffeyville, no, more like a brother. Along with Dan, who took care of my yard and helped with anything that was needed around the house, loaded everything for me.

Making the right kind of friends can make all the difference in life. The wrong friends can lead you into a direction you would have never gone on your own. Just because someone is popular does not mean they are good. Just because someone is not popular does not mean they are bad. Choose your friends based on their character. If you look deep, you will see it.

I put all the cats in pet taxies and we left Coffeyville. It was a four hour drive to Russellville, Arkansas, but all the cats seem to tolerate it well. When we got to Arkansas, we took them straight to the FROG (Family Room Over the Garage). We turned them loose and they seemed OK. Blacky could not go out every night like she did in Coffeyville, but it didn't seem to bother her. All her Kiddy Kats were together and safe, that's all that mattered. She just stayed with them now, all the time. That's when she became a true Mommy Kitty Kat.

THE MOVE CONTINUED

We would take the baby Kiddie Kats into the back yard every afternoon when the weather was nice. They were so young and would not go far. Blacky was nervous and didn't know the area so she would not go far. She had become a true Mommy Kat by this time.

My wife said she had seen what happens to cats and she would not let any of them go until they had been spayed or neutered. So, we kept them all for six months. Now they had had all their shots and been spayed or neutered.

At that point I began to lose them.

I let Ramous go to Shelby. He was the only big fuzzy cat. We named him after Ramous, from the movie "The Hunt for Red October". He was the biggest of all the cats. Shelby was also a scrub tech that I worked with and trusted. I knew she and her family would take such good care of him. My wife was so afraid. She cried and cried. She sent a letter with the cat saying that if any time they didn't want him we would take him back. But again, we are back to trust. I trusted Shelby and her family. They would never go back on their word, never. So I let him go !!!!

We loved these Kiddie Kats so much.

Next was Dottie. She was a tuxedo cat. She had a black dot on the back of each of her white back legs. That's why we called her Dottie. She was kind of afraid of everything, so I was worried most about her. She went to Rachelle. Remember, she was the scrub tech that also worked at the Yoke and volunteered at Burn Camp each year. She had been so kind to keep all of them so many weekends. I knew she would protect her the most.

At this point I just couldn't let go of any more of my Kiddie Kats. I didn't need a mommy cat with three kittens. But remember, I had promised Blacky I would always take care of her. So that means her kittens too.

I still had Maximus. He was a tuxedo cat with a pink nose. He had silky black and white fur. Avery, my oldest granddaughter would say to him "Maximus, you're too pretty to be a boy". He was the hunter and bird killer. He was named after Maximus from the movie, "Gladiator".

Then Indiana, Indiana Jones, the explorer. He was a striped cat. He had tan fur with perfect black stripes. He would explore everywhere. He is always the last to come in. He would search everywhere and loves to climb trees.

And then there was the last cat. She really would not let me or my wife touch her. We could never pick her up. She was the only female left, so she seemed to be kind of "left out". But as soon as Avery, my oldest granddaughter, came in and saw her for the first time, she picked up that last cat. The cat that no one else could pick up. No one else could touch. And that last cat just draped herself around Avery and Avery draped herself around her. She was a black cat, like Blacky, so, of course, she named her Strawberry.

THE LAST MOVE

I never intended to move again in my life. In fact I always said to people "my next move will be to a nursing home". But I had rental property and one of my renters had a pet delivery service. They drove pets all over the nation. He came to me and said he would like to stop traveling and open a pet day care. Well, I told my real estate agent about this and we found a few properties then she sent me this one as a joke. "Oh, this would make a nice pet day care!!!!" And so I made the mistake of showing it to my wife and then going to look at it ourselves. We knew as soon as we saw it, it would become the Kiddy Kat Ranch.

We moved there. Now Blacky and the last three Kiddy Kat's live there in peace. They stay in the laundry room. It has a doggy/cat door that leads out into and out of an oversized two car garage. After I feed them in the morning, we go outside for the Kiddy Kat walk.

Now every morning we go on the Kiddy Kat walk. I sing to them, "Now we live on the Kiddy Kat Ranch, we're raising cats in the old pea patch. Where the cats are fat and they're not going back,,,,,,,,, to Coffeyville where they lived as alley cats...... Cause now they live on a Kiddy Kat Ranch".

We always go down to the pavilion, then maybe down to feed the Kiddy Kat Fish in the lake, or up into the forest, (that's their favorite). But when I sing to them, they come, and when I stop, they stop. I was the first voice they heard in life. And they all pushed their way through that chain link fence that they really couldn't fit though just to find my voice.

Blacky is always just a step behind. Always watching. She has lived on the streets. She knows that it is dangerous out there. She is always watching out for her baby Kiddy Kats!!!!! She is a good Mommy Cat.

I guess good things do come to those who wait !! Blacky waited, I have to believe her owner was someone that could no longer take of a cat. And no one wanted her cat. I think Blacky lived and fought on the streets, waiting and believing there was someone out there that would love her and provide her a good home. She waited and she found me.

I waited for my wife, and I finally found her and knew she was the one that would love me forever. I waited and my wife waited for me, and we found each other.

God really does have a plan for all of us. Do you have the patience to see it out ?? Do you have the trust to believe it is real ??? Have you made the kind of friends you can depend on

??? Are you willing to trust enough to give up what you love for what you know is best ???

These are the hardest questions in life. You will have to answer them in your own life. God will help if you will let him. He is there. All you have to do is ask, and believe………..